MW01129852

Private Label Empire Build a Brand – Launch On Amazon FBA

Eli C Gordon

Copyright 2016 by Eli C. Gordon - All rights reserved.

This document is geared towards providing exact and reliable information in regards to the topic and issue covered. The publication is sold with the idea that the publisher is not required to render accounting, officially permitted, or otherwise, qualified services. If advice is necessary, legal or professional, a practiced individual in the profession should be ordered.

- From a Declaration of Principles which was accepted and approved equally by a Committee of the American Bar Association and a Committee of Publishers and Associations.

In no way is it legal to reproduce, duplicate, or transmit any part of this document in either electronic means or in printed format. Recording of this publication is strictly prohibited and any storage of this document is not allowed unless with written permission from the publisher. All rights reserved.

The information provided herein is stated to be truthful and consistent, in that any liability, in terms of inattention or otherwise, by any usage or abuse of any policies, processes, or directions contained within is the solitary and utter responsibility of the recipient reader. Under no circumstances will any legal responsibility or blame be held against the publisher for any reparation, damages, or monetary loss due to the information herein, either directly or indirectly.

Respective authors own all copyrights not held by the publisher.

The information herein is offered for informational purposes solely, and is universal as so. The presentation of the information is without contract or any type of guarantee assurance.

The trademarks that are used are without any consent, and the publication of the trademark is without permission or backing by the trademark owner. All trademarks and brands within this book are for clarifying purposes only and are the owned by the owners themselves, not affiliated with this document.

Contents

Introduction

Have you been looking for a way to create a home based business online? But you see the enormous amount of work to create your own website, drive traffic, fulfill orders (if you are lucky enough to get any) and provide all the customer service yourself. Sounds like a nightmare to me. And a risky one at that.

But there is another way....

Amazon has created the perfect channel to take advantage of the online world, without all the hassles of doing it all yourself. Amazon is a mammoth in the online world. Amazon.com has millions of unique visitors every year, with over 200 million credit cards on file.

Do you know anyone who hasn't shopped on amazon?

Amazon created their fulfillment centers (commonly known as FBA or Fulfillment by Amazon) to provide quicker delivery to the customers; but they are also a unique idea to solve every online marketers' problem of selling online. We all like the idea of using the internet to sell products, but are all less enthusiastic about stocking our basements, and then, when we each order comes in, packaging it, sending it with UPS, etc. The fulfillment centers solve the biggest headache of selling online by taking care of all that for you. You send the products to Amazon's warehouse and they take care of all the distribution. The fee for this service varies depending on the product, but averages about 25%. I will gladly give up 25% to get in front of the largest marketplace in the world and to not have to worry about that part of the business. Online sellers have quickly embraced this new system. We have realized, that compared with Ebay, this allows us more time to focus on finding products to sell and the benefits far outweigh the meager 25% taken by Amazon to do all the dirty work.

Amazon sellers generally fall into two camps with this FBA model. The first group is what we call "arbitrageurs". They source products locally in discount bins, big box stores, flea markets, etc. They are looking for a great price on products that will sell on Amazon for a profit. They look for arbitrage deals, which is the difference between the price they pay and the price they can sell on Amazon. The difference between the two amounts, less Amazon fees, is their profit. This is a valid business model, but this book will not discuss this approach. If you are interested in learning more, search on Amazon for "selling on Amazon" with the word "arbitrage" and you will find plenty of books to teach you this approach.

The second group to embrace the Amazon system are the "private labelers". That is the focus of this book. Private labelers are looking to create their own brand. We source our products directly from the manufacturers or wholesalers, from anywhere in the world. We then create our own packaging and brand, our own logo and design, and then market the final product as our own. The advantage to this business model is that we are creating a real business by building our own brand. It is a business that can be built over time and even eventually sold. The "arbitrageurs" are fighting over the buy box on Amazon, but for us the only competition are the other brands being sold on Amazon.

This is a business model like no other! You can start with less than $5000 and build it from there. I will not promise you that it is always easy, but with enough effort it is something that anyone can do. This book is enough to give you a foundation to start on the path of building your own "real business" It will give you the tools you need to start down that road to financial independence. Each chapter will give you a step by step plan to keeping the business moving along until you have your first product on Amazon (which can be done in as little time as a month, but most commonly takes 90 days).

There are many courses on the market today that will teach you this method. Some of them cost up to $4000. They are excellent courses and some of you may choose to purchase them to accelerate your learning time. But you don't need to start there. All of the resources that you need to learn this business already online for free. This book will not be able to cover every tiny detail (which would probably take a couple thousand pages) but it will give you a basis to start from.

In my opinion, the greatest strength of the Amazing Selling Machine (I have never been a member) is not the content of the information but the community it gives. Success in this business is all about the 1000 tiny different details. In the resources section at the end of the book, I make a list of all the free podcasts, YouTube videos, Facebook pages etc. that you will need. With this book I will show you the basics and where to find that community, where you can ask questions.

If you have deep pockets, then the $4000 course may be the route to go, but my suggestion is to spend it on your first batch of inventory. Spending a couple thousand dollars on inventory and actually going through the process yourself will give the greatest education you can pay for.

Why this private label process is such an awesome business model?

Obviously, if you are already aware of the great potential this business has for you, don't hesitate to jump to chapter 2. But for those of you which are completely new to this opportunity, here is why I believe this is such fantastic opportunity...

Have you read the 4-hour Work Week by Tim Ferris? If not, place it as the next book on your "to read list". In it, Tim discuss building a lifestyle business. Not only a business that has the opportunity to earn lots of money, but one that can create a great lifestyle for you and your family. A business that allows you to work from anywhere, to travel the world and to spend time with your family. There are certain business models that allow for this type of lifestyle and the Amazon private label business is one of them.

Low Start Up Investment

To start, where can you find an opportunity with such a low starting investment cost? Most people start with an investment anywhere between $500 and $5000. It is your choice in how big you would like to start off. The initial cost of inventory can be less than $5000. Other than that, there are very few other costs involved in getting going. Just your time and effort. In Chapter 5, I will show you step by step how to source a product and have it shipped to Amazon.

Quick payback on your initial investment

When anyone starts a business, the first thing they should be thinking about is, "how long is it going to take to get my money back out of this investment?" If you watch Shark Tank, this is the recurring theme for each of the investors. With this business model, it will take a couple months (or less) of selling to recoup your capital costs. If you do things right, you have sold your first batch of inventory within the first two months. The profit margins (after Amazon fees etc.) average around 30-50%, meaning that if you invest $1000 in inventory, you will have made a profit of $500 and have $1000 back into your bank account within the first month or two. I always recommend that if you want to grow your business quickly, you keep reinvesting your profits back into the business for as long as possible. But even with that being said, within 6 to 12 months you can be paying yourself a healthy salary. How many brick and mortar businesses can promise you that?

Minimal Risk

Since the start-up cost is so low, that is really all that you have on the table, other than your time. If you screw something up, it will not send you into bankruptcy.

Huge passive income potential

Let me give you some simple math. Let's say that your first product averages $10 in profit for each sale. It is not unreasonable at all, if you follow the method that I show you, you are able to sell 15-25 units a day. This should take you between 30 and 90 days to get to that level. So.... $10 per unit profit X 20 units per day is $200 per day. $200 per day X 30 days per month = $6000 per month. I realize that you might not want to quit your day job just yet, and it took you a couple of months to get there, but what happens if you find one more product? Or five more? Or twenty more?

20 products X $6000 = $120,000 per month! Which leads me to my next point.

Scalability

We all know a business owner that is working 14 hour days, trying to grow his business but is stuck, because "he is the business". The business was able to grow to a certain size but then it stalled because it required more and more time of the business owner to keep going.

With the private label model, the heavy lifting is building the infrastructure in the beginning. Finding a product, arranging the shipping, and learning how Amazon works is the hardest part of the whole process. But once you are able to sell one batch of inventory, ordering the next one is easy. Once you have created one product, the next one is a 100 times easier.

Since Amazon is taking care of the distribution, your only job is fine tuning the Amazon listing (Chapter 7) and looking for the next product to bring into the brand. Once you have the cash flow from the first and second product, it is not unreasonable to start bringing several new products online each and every month. The sky's the limit on how big you are able to grow this business.

The size of Amazon and their brand loyalty

By partnering with Amazon, we have the biggest marketplace in the world at our fingertips. The opportunity to leverage their brand loyalty is enormous. People trust Amazon. They know that if they ever have any problems with a product they can return it within 30 days without any problems or hassles.

With FBA centers built all across the USA and Prime shipping, there are millions of customers that can buy from Amazon and have the product shipped to their home within 48 hours with no shipping cost. The sales of Amazon are growing double digits each year, and there is no sign of them stopping.

Can you see the potential?

Can you see the potential of this tremendous opportunity? Are you excited to learn more and find out whether you are up to the challenge? In the following chapters I will walk you through the process and you will find that it is not as complicated as you might think.

Chapter 1 The Vision

Where do I start? The Vision

To start, let me state my vision. I am building a large brand. Amazon is NOT my business. It is a platform to launch my brand. When I establish my first brand firmly, then I will build another brand. The number one mistake that new sellers make when building up their business is that they are looking for products to sell, rather than looking for a company to build. It does not make sense to start selling iPhone cases, then to start selling spatulas. That is not a brand. If you decide to start with iPhone cases, build a whole line of them, from every type of phone available. Amazon is the launch pad for a real company.

Your first product

There are several criteria that make up the "perfect first product", but please remember that it is unlikely to find ALL of them. You may find a couple of the criteria, but you will need to evaluate them all when you are making your decision.

There are a number of free tools and hacks available to estimate all of these criteria. There are also tools with a cost attached that savvy developers have created. Please visit my website for an updated list of the most current tools available.

Your Unique Situation

Everyone coming into this business is starting at a different place. There is no cookie cutter formula to follow to build a brand that will work for everyone. Let me give you a questions to noodle on:

1. How much available capital do you have to start?

2. What internet marketing background do you have?

I hope I am not overstating the obvious here, but I see a number people going into niches that they have no business being in, because they see hot products and other people doing well. The very first decision that a new seller needs to make is how much competition are they going to go after. Higher competition equals higher possible rewards, but also higher possible risk. Let me break it down, and I will start from the top:

Deep pockets, previous marketing experience, big balls:

You got deep pockets (over $50,000) and you have experience in the world of online business. I wonder if there is anyone in this category buying this book? I kind of doubt it. They will buy the $4000 course. Anyways, I digress, if this is you, there are categories that you can enter in Amazon where 6 months later you may be making $100,000 per month. These categories are highly competitive but highly profitable such as supplements and health and beauty. You can sell hundreds of units a day, but the competition is fierce and only those with deep pockets and guts survive. Everyone else gets killed!

So my point is this; be very careful of high competition products if you don't have the means to outwit and outmaneuver the sellers with more money and experience than you.

Over $10,000 in capital

You certainly do not need over $10,000 to start, but people in this category have a great opportunity to carve out their own success and create a brand on Amazon. It allows you order enough initial inventory to do promotions get your product ranked. It allows you enter into a moderately competitive products and to have the staying power to allow your product to rise to the top.

If this is your situation, I would say that you can comfortably look for products that sell in the BSR (Best Seller Rank) of 500 – 2500. You should look to order over 1000 units and create an aggressive launch strategy to rank your product quickly and stick the landing.

$5000 - $10,000 in Capital

Like the group above, you are still in good shape to launch a product. But the only difference would be that you must really plan out your launch strategy and be careful with the amount of inventory you buy. If you purchase too little, you may run out and lose your ranking.

I would suggest looking for moderately competitive products in the range of 1500 to 3000. You should really try to order at least 1000 units, so that you have enough to do your initial promotion and not run out of inventory before the next order.

Less than $5000

Absolutely you can make things work with less than $5000. But, I would say tread very lightly and carefully. You will have a lot of unique challenges if you try to private label a product. Without sufficient capital, your minimum order quantity will have to be small. You may get enticed to order inexpensive products and find out they are garbage. The biggest challenge is the large amount of competition of other small sellers that are in the less expensive markets as well. I didn't say it can't be done, it is just more challenging.

Product Criteria

Listed in no particular order, my criteria are:

1. BSR < 3000

The BSR (Bestsellers Sales Rank) is a rank of the sales volume for each product within its category. You will find the BSR ranking listing on each product under product details, along with its ranking in the subcategory. We are looking for a large market and hoping to carve out a small chunk of it.

Go to any product category on Amazon, and click on the Bestsellers tab. Amazon will show what sells best in each category. Start combing through each category and subcategory looking for products that catch your attention.

There are several things to look for. Is there just one hot selling product listed with a high BSR in the niche? Or do the #2 - #20 products have a good BSR too. Try to estimate the sales volume of the whole niche, to get a sense of how much you might be able to get.

Jungle Scout Chrome Extension
Check out www.junglescout.com to give a sense of the sales volume in each product category. If you are serious about getting

into this business model, Jungle Scout it an absolute must have tool. It will save you hours of research.

There are a couple versions of the tool. The Chrome extension allows you to scrape the data off the amazon searches. It will pull in all the relevant data into one table that will allow to access the viability of the product in seconds. Go to the website, where you will find demonstrations and examples of how it works.

One particular strategy that I find effective is to spy on other private label sellers. When you find a private label product, click on the seller's name that will bring you to their storefront. From there, run jungle scout to see if their other products are selling well. It is a strategy that will allow to find a number of products very fast.

Breadth of market

Look for products where you can sell at least 300 units sold per month. You also need to determine that there is sufficient volume within the category and that there is sufficient volume is distributed among about 10 sellers. For example, if you search for jumper cables, you will see:

Seller 1 – 700 units/mth –

Seller 2 – 500 units/mth

Seller 3 – 450 units/mth

Seller 4 – 400 units/mth

Etc.

The point is that you make sure there is volume of at least 3000 spread across the top 10 sellers. In your mind, you need to be confident that "if I can just get X number of reviews and rank number 4 for the keywords, I will sell 300 per month". You should be able to see that you can beat out other people by having a better listing, better images, better marketing, etc.

999 Free Trick to Estimate Sales Volume
If you want to get an estimate of what your potential competitors:

1) Choose an item (sold privately but listed FBA)

2) Add to cart

3) Edit Cart

4) Choose drop down for # of items to purchase

5) Click on "10+"

6) enter "999" - the largest number you can enter in this field. You can not have more than 1000 products in your checkout basket.

7) Click update

If the seller has less than 1,000 items in inventory, it will tell you - "This seller has only 657 of these available. To see if more are available from another seller, go to the product detail page" If you do this and Amazon accepts your 999, it means that the seller has more than 1000 in inventory. Choose another product and try again.

If the seller has less than 999, note the number. Come back every day at the same time for a week (or the same time a few days later) and check the number available. This will give you a good estimate of the units that are selling.

https://junglescout.com/ - will do this (and more) for a monthly fee.

2.   Price $15-40

We are looking for a product that has a price high enough to create some margin but a price that is not so high that we can't afford to buy inventory. There are certainly exceptions to this rule, but you will need to evaluate those according to your own budget.

3.   # of reviews is less than 500

Buyers are looking for social proof. They want to see others opinions on the product. But if your main competitor has 3000 five star reviews, it is going to be hard to compete against them. After you source your product and get it to Amazon, your number one concern is getting reviews. We will discuss this more in chapter 8, but it is a big consideration when you are evaluating the competition.

Unless you have deep pockets, don't go after heavy competition products with your first product. Select something that you feel you can compete against with less than 100 reviews.

4. Private Label potential

Look for a product that doesn't have household name brand. Usually these products are more generic in nature. Is there a brand name dog leash? I am not sure, as I am not a dog owner. Even if there are some well-respected brand names in the pet market, they are certainly not household names.

5. Small lightweight

Ideally the product is small and lightweight. In chapter 6 we will discuss the shipping options but obviously we want to spend the least amount possible on shipping. If the product comes from China, and you are able to send express (via air freight), the quicker you are in business, and the quicker you are able to replenish inventory.

Look for something less than 2 lbs but preferably less than 1 lbs.

6. Consumable

Again, in an ideal world, the product would be consumable. Think of any multilevel marketing company, they are all consumable products. With a consumable product that people enjoy, the customers just keep coming back for more, which makes for a much more stable and sustainable business. These products are mostly found in Health and Beauty, which is becoming more competitive.

7. Sourced in the USA

Most products will be eventually sourced in China because of the low costs. But if you can find the product in the USA, you don't need to worry about complicated shipping arrangements, customs, duties, FDA approvals, etc. and it will ultimately make the process much easier.

Remember that these are all suggestions and that it is unlikely that you will find a product that has all seven of these attributes.

Keep in mind that you need to strike a balance between finding a product with some of these attributes, without "doing what everyone else is doing". Please no more silicone baking mats or silicone oven mitts.!

Pitfalls

It is also important to be aware of various pitfalls.

Some new sellers get caught with these:

1. Patents

It is possible to get a counterfeit product from China that is exactly the same as a model found on Amazon. Double check that there are no patent infringements with the design before you place your order.

2. FDA approval / EPA regulations, etc.

Some products may be HAZMAT or need expensive testing to be sold in the US market. The last thing that you want is a product to get stuck in customs after you have paid for it.

3. Liability Issues

Consider carefully if there is a significant risk with someone suing you. Two areas that come to mind are baby products and some health products. We all need to carry liability insurance and having an incorporated company mitigates some of the risk, but a lawsuit is still not a process that any of us want to go through.

4. Seasonal Products

Obviously some products sell better in different times of the year. While you are analyzing products, be mindful of whether the high BSR is only a seasonal factor. It is fine if you want to sell seasonal products, but not OK to be stuck with 1000 units of ice scrapers in the middle of summer!

If you have concerns with any of the 4 cautions above, either look for another product that is more simple to bring to market or make sure that you speak with a qualified lawyer and liability insurance broker. I recommend that for your first product, BE VERY CAREFUL of these 4 cautions. Start with a simple product where you don't have to worry about it.

NEXT ACTIONS:

1.   Get Jungle Scout. It will save you hours of research. Start digging into the best seller categories and sub-categories. Look at other private label sellers and spy on what they are selling

2.   Block off a couple hours to spend on Amazon.

This doesn't need to be strenuous thinking time; any evening when you have an hour or two will be fine. Grab a notebook and pen, and start browsing through Amazon's different categories. What categories interest you the most?

Do you have a passion for cooking? If yes, then maybe all the kitchenware utensils might be an area that you could get into. Do you love animals? Then maybe pet supplies might be a good market? You get the point.

To start off, you are looking for products that sell well (BSR of less than 3000 in their category).

3.   When you find a market that interests you, build a list of 10 to 20 products to build a brand around. Explore a couple different categories and get a feel for some markets that you would consider entering.

Chapter 2 - The Brand

In this chapter I will be discussing the idea of building a brand. We want to build a company and establish a brand, not just sell individual products. You are looking for at least 10 to 20 products in a niche, in which you can build your brand.

As you are searching through the Amazon listings, looking for products to sell, be aware of the different brands that are there. Notice the packaging and the logos. Look for whether the competitors have multiple products in their niche.

As brand owners, you are looking to create your own unique selling proposition. What is the angle that will set your products apart from the rest? Is it your unique packaging? Or perhaps, it's something like your environmentally sustainable materials used in the product. Consider one of the greatest brands of all time, Apple. Steve Jobs was not concerned about making thousands of different products but was more concerned with making each product correctly. From the time an Apple customer opens the packaging to its end uses, the process is a unique experience.

SWOT analysis

As you are looking for a niche, do a SWOT analysis on the competition. The best place to find your information is in the customer reviews of the competition's products.

S stands for strengths. What is it that the competitors are doing well? Search the 4 and 5 star reviews to find what the customers like about their products. These are things you want to emulate in your product.

W stands for weakness Search the 1 and 2 star reviews to find what the customers are unhappy about. Is there a simple adjustment that you can make to your product or an additional feature that would make your product better? This part of your search will give valuable information to set yourself apart.

O stands for opportunity - What is the overall market landscape for your niche? Is the niche expanding or is it shrinking? I suggest using Google trends and looking for expanding markets. As an example of a poor trend, a couple of years ago Garcinia Cambogia was a hot topic because it was featured on the Dr Oz show. Sales for this product were exploding on Amazon, and everyone was looking to cash in on this hot market. Marketers saturated Amazon with a 1000 different options but now the excitement is fading and the craze is slowing dying. If you want to carve out a niche, look for a steady expanding market.

T stands for threats - What are the market threats for your niche? We want to build a long term sustainable business, not just create some quick sales in the next year. Is the niche in an area where technology is rapidly changing? Is there any risk to your product becoming obsolete in 5 years?

Strengths and weaknesses are internal to your product, while opportunities and threats are external to the overall market. Analyze each niche carefully and consider these four factors, as you try to pick out your product.

Features and Benefits of your product

Quality

As you sift through the competition's products, pay close attention to the apparent quality. Is it a product that you would buy? Does the listing's title, description and photos make you feel like you are getting a quality product? Ideally we are looking for niches that sell well, but where there is still some room for improvement, whether in the listing or the product itself.

Packaging

Packaging can have a huge impact on our perception of the product. Two products can be exactly the same but the one with superior packaging is perceived to be of higher quality. In Chapter 5 we discuss how you can make high quality packaging and stand out from the rest.

Price

As you look for the appropriate product to sell, notice the price points that are selling well in each niche. Where will you carve out your 10 to 30 sales a day? Look for opportunities in each niche to find a product to sell at a higher price point. What attributes and qualities does the product need to have to sell at the higher price point? Again, using the Apple example, do you want to go after the higher quality/higher price sales?

On the flip side, some sellers look to try to compete on a volume basis on the lower end of the price point. Is there any way that you can provide a high quality item at a really competitive price? In many cases, this may result in a lower profit margin on each unit sold. But if you can sell enough volume at a lower price, it still may be the most profitable to the bottom line.

There is no single strategy that is perfect in every scenario, but the cardinal rule is to not skimp on quality. If you do, you risk having customers unhappy, leaving poor reviews, and product returns.

NEXT ACTIONS

As you go through the Amazon listings, looking for a product, where do you see your brand fitting in? What will set yours apart from the rest?

Continue to make notes on product opportunities and try to narrow down your selections, to one or two niches that you are excited about exploring further.

Chapter 3 - Sourcing a product

The next step of the process, after you have identified some products (or perhaps while you are identifying them), is to source out potential suppliers that you can use to produce your own private label product. Before the internet came along, only those large multinational companies with the large Rolodex were able to source products from around the world. But with search engines that has all changed!

Alibaba

Just as Amazon is to the retail consumer, Alibaba is to the business to business community. With the same ease as Amazon, Alibaba allows us to communicate directly with the suppliers and wholesalers around the world that produce the goods. Get onto Alibaba, set up an account, and start searching around. If you are looking for a spatula, you will find enough to keep you busy for days!

I suggest that as you search, you only use those that have the "Gold Supplier" rating and "On site Check". Those two items verify that the business has been around for at least 2 years, and that Alibaba has done an on-site check, to verify that there is actually a warehouse and an operating business.

Early on in the process, verify the type of payment options the supplier accepts. Use either Paypal and Ali escrow for your first payment to protect yourself. If they say that they only accept T/T (telegraphic transfer) or Western Union don't risk it, find another supplier that does. Most prefer T/T and that is fine after your first order. If they complain about the Paypal fee, ask them to add it to the invoice.

Aliexpress

Although I recommend that you go to Alibaba first, Aliexpress is another great resource as well. Aliexpress is mainly for single or small orders, while Alibaba is for larger orders. But many of the same suppliers that are on Aliexpress can supply larger orders if asked.

Global Sources

Another great site like Alibaba. It is maybe not as popular as Alibaba, but you are sure to find some gems there as well.

ThomasNet

If you are looking to find suppliers in the United States, Thomas Net is a great resource.

Google

Type in "<product> + wholesaler, supplier", and again you will find pages of suppliers that will gladly produce your private label product. The majority of the suppliers on Alibaba are from China (although that is currently becoming more global each day).

Google can help you find access to suppliers in the USA.

MOQ - Minimum Order Quantity

Each supplier will state their minimum order quantity. I recommend that you use it as a barometer but not as a hard and fast rule. If they state 1000 but you can only afford 500, don't hesitate to ask, because the worst that can happen is that they say no.

The Inquiry Email

Making your first inquiry to a number of different suppliers, is the first major step in the business. It can be a little bit nerve racking for the first timer, because you may feel a bit like an imposter, even though you have the anonymity of the internet. But every business has to start somewhere so just jump in and get your feet wet.

Some sellers suggest that you need to fake it; that you are the Vice-President of Sourcing of a big company. Others suggest that you are better off to let them know that you are new, so that you don't get yourself into trouble pretending to understand something when you need to ask a question. You will find that a lot of suppliers will not respond to you if they think you are a small fish, so it is probably best to lead with some confidence, and then admit to your limited experience early in the process. There is no wrong way to approach it, but only a preference on your part as to how you would like to handle the new relationship. I suggest that with your first email, you make a good first impression and ask one or two good questions. Do not bombard them with 15 different questions.

They are less likely to respond if you do. Their initial communication with you should be a signal as to the future relationship. Give more consideration to those that respond promptly, with excellent English.

After making a favorites list of all the potential suppliers I am interested in, I send the email to all of them at once through Alibaba's system. Here is an example of an inquiry email that I have used. Use it and adapt it to whatever feels comfortable to you:

Hello,

I would like to get a sample of the <product> and am looking to make a <number> unit trial order.

Can you please provide me pricing for the following quantities as we expect to increase sales quickly: 500, 1000, 2000, 4000, 10000?

I'd also like to check a few options for modifications with you. Please price units with the following modifications if possible: <mod 1> <mod 2>

Thanks in advance

<Your Name>, Brand Manager

<Company Name>

Samples

After you narrow down your suppliers to a few that you might want to deal with, the next step is to start ordering samples. How you do this will depend on your time line and budget. Each sample will have a cost (maybe $40-$60) to have it shipped to you. It is recommended that you order various samples to find what suits you best and that you can compare the quality. Don't ever settle. If there is something not right about the product (especially if it involves its quality) move on and find something else. If there is a small detail that you wish were different, don't hesitate to ask for a modification.

NEXT ACTIONS:

1.   Set up an Alibaba and Aliexpress account.

2.   Start adding favorites to your list.

3.   Send an inquiry email.

4.   Order samples.

Chapter 4 - Creating a brand

Note:

I suggest that you work on this section when you have the samples ordered. There is no point in worrying about any of these details until you are at least somewhat confident what your first product will be.

Naming the Company

This part for me was actually quite tricky. When you pick something, you want to make sure the website domain name is available. We went through probably 20 great names that were already taken before we settled on something. It is like naming your first born child.

There are various ways or styles to name a business. What is the feel you are trying to create? Think of a brand name that you would like to emulate. What is it that you like about it? Is it short and concise or is it descriptive? Use a thesaurus to look up synonyms and see if you can't find something there. I suggest you Google "how to name a business" to find some good help. Here are some recommendations to get you started with the process:

1. It needs to sound good, and is easy to remember. Consider alliteration (words that start with the same consonant) or rhyming

words if you use two words. Think Lululemon or Coca-Cola.

2.   Perhaps try the more descriptive angle but avoid making it too long.

3.   Get other people to help you and start brainstorming

4.   Try variations of words, or changing one letter (like a S to Z or F to PH)

Cautions:

Check that you can trademark your name. Visit USPTO.gov or a site called Trademarkia.com. Also check that you can get the web address for the name. Use a web hosting site like www.godaddy.com to check whether it is taken.

Website Domain Name
I hesitate to add this section here, for fear that you might go out and start creating a website. That is not what you should do! But you should make sure that your brand name is available, by going to go daddy etc. and buying you domain name.

After you have your products all picked out and into the Amazon system, and they are selling well, then (and only then) consider spending time creating a website.

Logo

The logo is the next most important item of your brand. It gives customers a picture of who you are. There are various sites to outsource this on the internet for a very low cost. I sent mine to 3 different graphic designers on fiverr.com and was able get two back that I really liked. After I made my decision, it cost me less than $25.

Other options include:

www.upwork.com

www.99designs.com

Packaging

Depending on the type of product that you go with, it will change what you choose for packaging. Some sellers go all out and create beautiful custom packaging to differentiate themselves from the competition. Other sellers take a "white label" approach to start. White label is where you do very little to the packaging other than put a simple label on the product. Packaging is important to the overall sales process, but I caution you not to get too hung up on it to start. If you can make a simple package design to start, that is great. Then improve it later when you have sales coming in.

Ask the supplier what packaging templates they have available. Most of them provide at least some sort of basic packaging as part of the cost. I have done my packaging designs with a graphic designer I have found in Central America off of elance.com. The designs are great, the communication is easy and the cost is very affordable.

You can use Fiverr and get something fairly basic for $5. Or you can try Upwork and put your product up for bid (this may cost $30 to $200 depending on the work). I have not yet used 99designs but I have heard that it is also very good.

NEXT ACTIONS:
1. Brainstorm 5 good names, and pick 1.

2. Make sure the domain name is not taken.

3. Create a logo.

4. Create unique packaging for your product.

Chapter 5 Cash flow projections - know your numbers

Rule #1 as a business owner, you must know your numbers. You should know your cost of goods sold, your profit margins, and advertising costs, like the back of your hand. At the start of the business you must be continually reinvesting profits into the business. If you do it right, the reinvested money should have a huge return on investment, and you are able to ramp up the business fast.

When selecting a product, you must be constantly running the numbers with your cash flow projections. There are numerous variables that can change with each scenario. Price, shipping cost, quantity, PPC promotions, etc. all play a factor in your overall profit and margin.

Having a spreadsheet where you can play with the numbers is an absolute must if you are going to out strategize the competition.

When I launch each product, I am constantly thinking of how I will outpace the competitors. The strategies in this book will give you the tools in the tool belt, but it is up to you to apply them in the most effective way possible. The strategies that you use will be dependent on your unique product and the market that you are in.

In the beginning when you are sourcing products it is imperative that you analyze the numbers, weighing all your different options. Rule of thumb is to look for a product where you can sell for at least 3 times the price of its Manufactured cost (plus shipping). This will allow you to have enough margin in the beginning to do promotions, discounts, etc.

Chapter 6 - Shipping and Inspection

Air vs Sea

If you are shipping internationally, the easiest method by far is to have the products shipped by the supplier via air (the Chinese call this Air Express shipping). You can be in business quickly because it takes only about a week to get it to Amazon but the cost via air can be double the what you might pay if you ship it by vessel (sea).

Shipping by sea can take over a month (40 days) and you will want to organize the shipping with a freight forwarder. The time spent waiting while the product is in the middle of the Pacific can be painful. It is much harder to manage your inventory when you have a month delay time with just shipping (not to mention the lead time needed to produce the products).

A seller needs to weigh these costs and constraints carefully when making the business plan. Shipping by vessel can save lots of money, which can later allow you to compete much more aggressively on price as you are building the brand. But on the other hand, if it causes you to run out of inventory, what is the cost of that?

If you pick a product that is small and light, choose express shipping to start. When you figure out your sales volumes and have a bit of equity built up to get bigger inventories, then switch to vessel. If you have a larger or heavier product, you will have no choice but to choose sea freight.

Freight Forwarder

If you need to use sea shipping, your freight forwarder will become your best friend. Choose this relationship wisely. They coordinate everything between the supplier and the shipping company, they handle the importation process and customs, and the shipping to the Amazon warehouse. It is important that they understand the requirements of Amazon such as the labeling requirements, size requirements and pallet requirements. Ask the freight forwarders that you interview whether they have experience shipping to Amazon.

Inspection Services

Some sellers choose to add this step into the process and some do not. The risk of not having an inspection of the inventory, can be a disaster if faulty products start getting sold from Amazon. If you live in the United States, it is best to have the products shipped to your home first, at least for the first shipment and until you become comfortable with the quality control of the supplier.

Alternatively, if you search on Alibaba or Upwork you can also find inspection services in China. They will visit the factory for you and inspect the final product before it is shipped.

Labeling

All products shipped to Amazon need to have a label. If you don't want to do it yourself, you can pay Amazon to do it for you. If you are only selling on Amazon, then you can use their FNSKU number and have that code placed on the product to avoid having to put stickers on each item. The other option is using the "commingled inventory" with Amazon and use a UPC code. This would allow you to use the same UPC code (and keep the packaging the same) if you plan to sell the item on other sites beyond Amazon.

Inventory Placement Services

When you create your shipment to send to Amazon, their algorithm will determine where you need to send your inventory. The algorithm frequently determines (based on sales volumes and other factors) that you need to send your inventory to two or more different fulfillment centers. Obviously this creates an added cost to your shipping plan. As an alternative, you can choose to enable the inventory placement services of Amazon. With this plan you send all of your inventory to one fulfillment center location and then Amazon ships it to other locations for a fee. The fee varies depending on weights and sizes. Since you can either choose to use this service or not, you need to figure which is the cheapest option for you; whether to ship to one location and have Amazon charge you to move it around or to have the inventory shipped directly to the various locations. I recommend that you analyze each option, because the cost can vary by several hundred dollars depending on the variables involved.

NEXT ACTIONS:

1. Decide whether you will use Air Express or Vessel.

2. Arrange a freight forwarder if necessary.

3. Figure out your plan for labeling.

4. Determine whether using the Inventory Placement option OR shipping to multiple FBA centers is less expensive.

Chapter 7 The Listing

Here is where marketers finally start to have some fun! The listing is your opportunity to show the world how your product is better than all the rest.

Customers search Amazon with the search engine. Amazon will show the bestselling and most relevant products first in the search. So here is list of the most important variables involved.

Keywords

Like Google, Amazon uses words in your title, bullet points and description field to match the customers search. You want to make sure that you have as many of those keywords as possible in your listing. Explore the listings of your competitors to see what keywords they are using and look at merchantwords.com to see the search volume for those keywords. Consider complementary products that customers might buy at the same time as they buy yours. Place those keywords into the listing so you will show up on those searches too.

There are a number of websites that that help with keyword research. All of these I have used:

www.merchantwords.com

www.scientificseller.com

www.keywordinspector.com

www.helium10.com

These tools are a great way to research the possible keywords and estimate traffic. Don't assume just because you would find a product by using a particular phrase, all other buyers will use the same phrase of keywords. There will be hundreds of different keyword combinations to find the same product. Use the tools above to find all these keyword combinations.

Place your best keywords in your title. Then place them in your bullet points and description. For any keywords that you can't place into the main part of your listing, place them in the "back end". There is place in the listing setup page that allows you to add another 5000 character of keywords. Don't feel obligated to fill it all up, but make sure that all of the keywords are relevant to your listing.

Spanish Keywords and Common Mis-spellings

For your main keywords, find the Spanish equivalents. Also find the main miss-spellings for your main keywords, and place them in the back end. A lot of sellers don't do this, but it may add another couple sales a week to your sales.

Listing Optimization

When your product is up a selling, there is a tendency to try to perfect your listing. This is fine as long as you don't fiddle with it too much. My suggestion is to make changes only once per week, and to make only one major change each time. If you make too many changes and make them too often, it is hard to determine what factors are influencing your conversion rate. There is no way to split test the variables, so we need to be patient and test each variable one at a time.

Bullet Points - Features and Benefits

Customers are interested in the features of the product, but they BUY their benefits. New sellers like to list the features of the products but forget to add the benefits to the end user. You need to sell the benefits of your product and have a call to action.

Conversion Rate

When someone finds your product and they click on the listing, what percentage of them buy your product? If the conversion rate is low (IE less than 10%) it means that people are not liking what they are seeing. If you have a good conversion rate (IE 20% to 30%) it means that when customers find your product, a good portion of them are satisfied to not look any further.

Remember, a big factor in your conversion rate is the number of reviews that you have. Your conversion rate will get better as you increase the number of positive reviews in your listing.

Click through rate

The click through rate is the percentage of time that customers see your item (impressions) and click on the listing to explore it more. Amazon wants place products in front of customers that have higher click through rates. This is a determining factor if you are using pay per click advertising, discussed later.

One of the most important parts of the listing is the pictures that you choose. Since there is not a physical product for them to hold in their hands, customers spend a lot of time studying the picture. Make sure your photos are of the highest quality possible and use all of the 9 available spots.

I could go on and on about improving the listing but the best learning will come as you study the competitor's listings in your niche. Look at the things that you like and don't like. Study their sales copy and call to action. Don't copy someone else's listing, but use it as a base to make your own even better.

NEXT ACTIONS:

1. Study the sales copy of the competition.

2. Create a compelling listing, with a strong title and bullet points.

3. Obtain high quality photos. (make sure they are within Amazon TOS)

4. When you are up and running, make optimization

improvements once per week.

Chapter 8 - The Launch

Yeah! You finally are in business. You got your product to Amazon, the listing is perfected and you are listed on page 15 of the keywords search. No one knows you are there and you have no sales!

You have to have a plan to launch your product so that you start climbing up the rank on the keyword searches. Sales and reviews are all you should be worrying about at this stage. Don't worry about your website, your next product, or the million other things out there to fiddle with. You just need to get sales and reviews.

Family and Friends

The first step is to set up a promotion so that you can sell products to your friends and family. I recommend this with caution. This is the current guidelines from Amazon:

"Promotional Reviews – In order to preserve the integrity of Customer Reviews, we do not permit artists, authors, developers, manufacturers, publishers, sellers or vendors to write Customer Reviews for their own products or services, to post negative reviews on competing products or services, or to vote on the helpfulness of reviews. For the same reason, family members or close friends of the person, group, or company selling on Amazon may not write Customer Reviews for those particular items."

"Paid Reviews – We do not permit reviews or votes on the helpfulness of reviews that are posted in exchange for compensation of any kind, including payment (whether in the form of money or gift certificates), bonus content, entry to a contest or sweepstakes, discounts on future purchases, extra product, or other gifts.

The sole exception to this rule is when a free or discounted copy of a physical product is provided to a customer up front. In this case, if you offer a free or discounted product in exchange for a review, you must clearly state that you welcome both positive and negative feedback. If you receive a free or discounted product in exchange for your review, you must clearly and conspicuously disclose that fact. Reviews from the Amazon Vine program are already labeled, so additional disclosure is not necessary."

Amazon determines that "close friends or family" as anyone that you have ever received a product from or has received a product from you. Regardless, there are always at least 10 to 20 reviews that you can get from your circle of influence. Start there. You will have very few sales until you get at least 10 reviews.

Promo Codes

In order to get the snowball rolling down the hill, we need to give it a push to get it going. Promotional giveaways are going to be the best way to boost your sales and start climbing up the charts for your keyword searches.

A coupon code allows you to offer a low price (IE $1 to $4.99) to give away product in exchange for honest reviews. There are various methods to do this and some are more "black hat" than others, so be careful not to cross the lines of Amazon's Terms of Service. In the future it is predicted that Amazon will find ways to crack down on dishonestly obtained reviews, so be careful in which method you obtain them.

The object of these promotions is to spike Amazon's algorithm with sales, to help you climb rankings for your keywords and also as a way to generate more reviews. As you climb the BSR rate with the promotion, you also start to get organic sales. You need to do this consistently enough in the beginning until you start to naturally start getting organic sales to be on page one for your keyword searches.

There are various sites that you can do these launches. This is only a partial list:

www.zonblast.com has a large list that will quickly buy your promo and are well trained to leave reviews.

www.tomoson.com - A site to target bloggers.

www.reviewkick.com

There are numerous Facebook groups that offer promotion services if you start searching. My main caution is that you be careful of them crossing over the line of the Amazon Terms of Service.

Pay per Click

After you have more than 15-20 reviews (this number will depend on the niche), you can now start advertising with Amazon pay per click. The reviews are needed for social proof, so that your conversion rate is high enough to justify the cost per click. Spend as much as you can comfortably afford. Just like the promotions, this advertising is not intended to help make you profitable just yet, but to help you climb the BSR and searches for keywords so that you can start getting organic sales.

When you first set up PPC, start by running a test campaign using the AUTO setting and let Amazon target keywords for you. Then let it run on AUTO for a week and analyze the results. Amazon's algorithm will work to spend your budget and will target keywords to increase the number of sales. You will be surprised that it will find keywords that you will not have considered. Now switch PPC to manual, and target the keywords that are most profitable.

When you are in the planning stages (ordering products etc.) consider carefully the costs of the promotions and PPC advertising. Sellers that fail and drop out of this business expect to be getting organic sales from day one. It doesn't happen like that. The amount you spend on promotion and advertising will depend on the competitiveness of your niche. Estimate how much you will need to promote your product to get a similar number of reviews as your competitors. Like any business, you need to spend a bit at the beginning to get it moving.

Manual PPC Campaigns

In addition to the auto campaign that you set up, you will also want to set up manual campaigns. There are three types, Broad Match, Phrase Match and Exact Match.

Broad Match example – red shoes. In this case it would be advertised to any match that has both the words red and shoes in the search. For example, best red sport shoes, or best red shoes for basketball

Phrase Match – The keywords "red shoes" need to be together in the search. For example, "best red shoes" or "red shoes for basketball"

Exact Match- The keywords have to be exactly the same. Only a search for "red shoes" will show up.

My strategy is to create campaigns (not ad groups) for Auto, Broad, Phrase and Exact. By setting them up at the campaign level, it allows me to manage my budget for each, separately.

I will create all the possible keyword matches from a site like scientificseller.com and then dump them into the Broad, Phrase, and Exact campaigns. I turn them on with a moderate budget and monitor them over the next few weeks. I will cut out the obvious losers right away, but for most of the keywords I will let them run for a few weeks. At that point, I will start adjusting the bid prices and removing obvious losers.

www.ppcscope.com is a tool that I now use to monitor my ppc campaigns. Brian Johnson, the creator of PPCscope has some great training on the area of ppc optimization, so when you get to that point, I highly suggest researching his suggestions and recommendations.

Holding Inventory

If you plan to do a promotional give away, where you plan to distribute a promo code, it is absolutely imperative that you protect your inventory. There have been numerous rookie sellers that have lost major portions of their inventories because their promo code got leaked onto a blog.

To prevent this from happening, follow these steps:

1. Create a Fulfillment order to yourself for the amount of product that you want to protect. If you have 500 units, and you only want to give 50 coupons, make the fulfillment order for 450.

2. Set the order on hold for two weeks rather than ship it.

3.   Ensure the code is exclusive and good for 1 single purchase only.

4.   Cancel the promo code when the promotion is over.

5.   Cancel the shipment to yourself when the promotion is over. This takes 2 or 3 minutes for the inventory to be available again.

Be careful to make sure to keep the coupon private. There is an option to post the coupon on the Amazon listing (usually used to offer 2 for 1, or small discounts). If this option is selected, and your coupon is significant, it is visible to everyone, and your inventory can be gone in minutes.

Reviews

Remember paying Monopoly? Who is the one who always wins? The person with the most houses. In Monopoly you don't have time to be picky; you just buy every property that you can, and be as aggressive as possible buying houses. Then you hope for the best. Usually, the player that is most aggressive with this strategy (coupled with a bit of luck) wins.

In the Amazon world, "He who has the most reviews wins." Reviews are the name of the game PERIOD. In the beginning, if you are not placing the majority of you focus on getting more reviews than the competition you are missing the point.

More reviews and better reviews = higher conversion rate

Without reviews, your conversion rate will suffer. If you are running PPC, that means you will spend more. If your conversion rate sucks, it will be hard to stay on the front page.

The first thing you must do to increase reviews, is start asking for them. Using review software is an absolute must if you want to be serious about getting more reviews.

Some recommended services for getting product reviews are:

www.salesbacker.com

www.feedbackgenius.com

Very few people will naturally give you reviews and the ones that do will usually be the people that are unhappy about something. Reviews and social proof are the lifeblood of your business and you need to focus all your time and energy into generating reviews until you have more than your competitors. The only way to do this, is by asking for them. Amazon does not give you the customers email address, but they allow you to interact with them through their interface. There are several companies such as feedbackfive.com and feedbackgenius.com that have created software to optimize this process.

Once you have more than 50 reviews, and your listing is optimized, you should now be getting consistent organic sales. At this point you are finally making money and can start looking at adding a second product.

Secondary nodes

When you set up a listing, you are able to select the category that you wish for your product. But have you noticed that other sellers have two categories? These are called nodes.

This is a strategy to pick up an #1 Seller badge in a related (but smaller) category.

You are able to contact seller support, and request that want your product listed in another category. This is where it becomes very important to choose the right category. When buyers are looking for products they do not use the categories, but only the search tool. So having your product in another category will help you very little, UNLESS you have a #1 Seller badge.

I use my secondary listing to grab a #1 seller badge in a less competitive category. I look for a closely related category in which the #1 position has a higher BSR than I do. That way, when I get that secondary listing, I will pick up a #1 seller badge.

This is a top strategy because when shoppers a looking at your listing, they are much more likely to buy if it has a #1 seller badge, therefore increasing your conversion rates. This will improve your PPC as well.

Note that not all categories have a #1 Seller badge. The category must have at least 100 products. If it doesn't have 100 products, the #1 position will only get a XXXX badge.

Chapter 9 Customer Service

At the core of any sustainable business model is a strong emphasis on providing superior customer service. Amazon is recognized for outstanding customer service, and they expect that we uphold that image.

It is important to consider the life time value of a client. If they come back and order from you again, that is a tremendous uplift to your bottom line. The success of your brand will be determined by the quality of your reviews. Too many negative reviews will destroy your image and your sales.

I recommend setting up an email sequence to defend against any unhappy customers. It is easier to fix a problem at the beginning, rather than to deal with it after it has already blown up (on your reviews).

The first step of this process is to send an email immediately after the purchase:

Email #1
Dear <Customer>,

Thank you for ordering the <product>.

The product is being shipped today from the Amazon warehouse, and should arrive at your home within the next couple days.

At <company name> we pride ourselves in providing the highest quality products to our customers. We stand by our products 100%. If you are not completely satisfied for any reason, please contact us through the Amazon order system, and we promise to resolve any concerns.

One tip (IE make sure to wash it first etc.)

thank you,

<name> Owner

<company>

This email will allow you to address any problems in the beginning, hopefully before they leave any negative reviews.

The second email (5 days later)

Dear <Customer>

THANK YOU for your recent purchase of <product name>.

Your satisfaction is very important to us! We are a small, family run company, trying to compete against larger multinational brands. We try to do this by providing high quality products, at affordable prices.

We want to ensure that you are completely satisfied. If you have any questions, or if there is anything we can do to help, please let us know.

Reviews are absolutely HUGE on Amazon. They are THE KEY to really helping our company grow, and for our products to be seen on Amazon.

If you feel satisfied with your purchase, your positive review would be greatly appreciated.

If you have left a review already, THANK YOU VERY MUCH! If not, it will only take a couple of seconds.

Just click the link below and tell Amazon

what your experience has been with the <product>

<link>

THANK YOU

<name> Owner

<company name>

You may choose to send another email (similar to the second email) 12-15 days after purchase. Your review sequence may need to be adjusted because of the type of product that it is. For example, a supplement may need to be taken for several weeks before the customer feels comfortable leaving an honest review.

Negative Reviews

There will always be a certain portion of people on the planet that will be hard to please. Use the review email sequence to allow them to deal with you directly before leaving a review.

But if you do get bad reviews (and you will), the key to mitigating the effects of negative reviews is to get a sufficient quantity of positive reviews to outweigh them on your overall ranking. If you don't have any process to solicit positive reviews, your overall rating will suffer.

But in addition to that, you must do everything in your power to fix their problem. Communicate with them, reimburse them, etc. If you can fix the problem and satisfy them, they may voluntarily remove the negative review.

DO NOT bribe them, as it will go against Amazon's Terms of Service.

Seller Feedback Vs Product Review

In order to establish your strategy for reviews, it is first important to understand the current platform at Amazon. There are two places for buyers to leave feedback.

Seller Feedback

Seller Feedback is there for the buyer to rate your performance as a seller. It has nothing to do with the product. Seller feedback is there to rate your performance on shipping, customer services, etc.

Since some sellers on Amazon choose to ship the goods themselves, this feedback is important. But in the FBA world it is technically irrelevant, because Amazon takes care of all of those details.

Product Review

In the Private Label business, this is where the rubber meets the road. These are the reviews that the majority of buyers will be looking at.

Just Product reviews or both?

In the private label business, there are two main strategies to get reviews. I will explain both of them and give you the pros and cons.

The majority of sellers just go after the product review only. The reason why is obvious because the product reviews are the ones that really matter to buyers. You set up a review sequence of 3 emails to solicit reviews.

The second strategy is to go after both seller feedback and product reviews. The theory is that Seller Feedback is important to Amazon and will factor into the ranking process. Since no one knows that currently ranking algorithm at Amazon, it is hard to know for sure if this is how it works.

But the second reason for soliciting Seller Feedback first is that it allows you to screen for negative product reviews. Most buyers do not understand the difference between Seller Feedback and a Product Review. If we are asking for their Seller Feedback first, and they have a product complaint, they will often place that negative feedback in the Seller Feedback. The current Amazon policy states if someone leaves negative "product related" feedback in your Seller Feedback, it can be removed. This strategy allows you catch the problem before it gets to the more noticeable Product Review.

If on the other hand, the buyer leaves positive feedback in the Seller Feedback, it allows you to go ahead with confidence, asking for the Product Review. The process to do this with this strategy is to manually sent them another message (through the Amazon system) asking them to also leave a product review. Expect to get about 60-70% of the buyers that have given positive Seller Feedback to go the next step and leave a Product Review.

Pros and Cons
The pros of just going after a Product Review is that it is simple and will likely result in more overall reviews. But the Cons are that it is likely that you will get more negative product reviews.

If you choose the 2 step method of going after Seller Feedback first and then a Product review second, you are able to screen for negative product reviews.

Unverified vs Verified reviews

A verified review is one where the customer has purchased the product through Amazon. But Amazon also allows for unverified reviews as well. Hypothetically a person could buy a product at Walmart and then go onto Amazon and leave a review.

Most amazon sellers get all bent out of shape trying to get only verified reviews. It can be a pain sometimes if you are getting friends or bloggers to review a product and purchase it with the coupon code etc. You need them to buy it, then ship it, wait a few days, then remind them to leave a review.

I am not suggesting that you don't try to get verified reviews, but what I am saying is don't worry if some of them are unverified. If that is the quickest and easiest way to get those initial reviews, do it.

Most customers on Amazon do not understand the difference between a verified review or an unverified review. They don't really care that much, only we do.

Vote up good reviews / Vote down negative reviews

As you start to get reviews, some will be more helpful than others. A great strategy is to "vote up" good quality reviews. Buyers generally do not read all the reviews, but they will read the 1-3 most helpful reviews.

Amazon gives customers (buying or non buying) the ability to state whether they think a review is helpful or not. So the strategy is to get all your friends and family to "vote up" any good reviews (not necessarily 5 star) and "vote down" any negative reviews.

The goal is to not have any negative reviews showing on the first page, and have one solid (helpful) review showing as the first review people see.

Chapter 10 -Other Strategies

Postcard Insert

Since you are building a brand, you want be able to start to monetize the back end sales of each customer. All product niches are different and this approach may work better with some. The idea is to increase the lifetime value of each customer. One of the ways to do that is to either direct them to your other products or provide incentives for the m to purchase more of the current product from you in the future.

The end goal is to collect the customer's email address and the permission to market to them in the future. In order to receive that email address, you need to offer something of value.

The strategy that I use is to place a postcard in the packaging of each product. You can either direct them to a warranty page on your website (where you then collect their email), or to offer some kind of incentive such as a VIP discount on future products.

The Warranty Approach

The warranty is a great approach because it adds added value to the customer. Amazon's return policy is 30 days, so if you want to provide protection beyond that you need to provide a manufacturer's warranty.

The postcard would direct them to a warranty page on your website, which in fact is also a squeeze page to receive permission to also market to them in the future. Keep in mind that this is not some trick to get their email address to make a quick buck and then never honor the warranty. The warranty that you offer should be a long term commitment on your part to provide service and value to your customer.

VIP club

The other approach that I use is an offer for them to be part of the VIP club. Basically it is an offer letting them know that they can enter to receive promotional discounts on all future products. So instead of having a long arduous process of launching a product with friends and family, etc. you are able to offer each new product to your email list. By having the email list, you are able to prepare them for each launch, and allow them to receive the products for a deep discount in exchange for an honest review

Both of these strategies allows you to build an email list of customers that are anxious to review your products. The launch process becomes increasingly easier as this list grows. DO NOT neglect building this email for too long in the early process of building the business because it becomes a huge benefit for every additional product that you role out.

You will need to set up a website and an email autoresponder, to gather emails. Suggestions include:

www.bluehost.com – for hosting a WordPress site

www.aweber.com – email autoresponder

www.mailchimp.com - free email autoresponder

www.getresponse.com – email autoresponder

2 for 1 discounts

2 for 1 discounts is another great strategy for adding value and selling more products. If you have a product where people would be happy to get a second one at a discount, then setting up a coupon for an additional purchase, is a "must do" strategy.

Several of my products need to be washed every so often. Customers are anxious to choose my brand, because they can by a second or third item at a discounts. This adds value in their eyes and extra sales for me. I make dozens of extra sales each month by providing a coupon code.

Set up the coupon code, and advertise it on the product description page (or title, bullets).

Combined Discounts

If you have multiple products within the same niche and brand, then combined discounts are another great strategy. For example, if you are selling a pairing knife and a cutting board, great a discount for them to be purchased together.

This is a great strategy to showcase your brand and to pick up extra sales. The customer may have already needed both items, but most of the time it is an impulse buy. They see value it picking up the second product and getting a great deal.

Bundles
A strategy borrowed from the arbitrage sellers, creating bundles is an effective strategy for separating yourself from the competition. You can either bundle with another product that you are selling on Amazon, or will a smaller add-on that you create just for the one product.

A lot of sellers add an eBook. I personally don't see a lot of value in this, but it may be better than nothing. My feeling is that you can do better than an eBook. The ancillary item does not need to be expensive but it should have some perceived value in addition to the main product.

Chapter 11 Go Big!!!

Now that you are selling 20 to 30 units a day and starting to get some cash flow in your business, it is now time to move to the next phase. The next step is adding another product and taking it through the same process. You will find that the second time is much easier because of all the acquired knowledge and experience. Each time that you roll out a new product and are able to double the sales of your business, you are able to grow exponentially. You now have sufficient cash flow to quickly promote your new products and blow away your competition. After the initial success of one product, it doesn't take long to scale up this business.

In the beginning it is important to build on the niche and the brand that you started. You will build synergy within the sales of your products. Customers will buy multiple products from you if they are happy with your brand.

But after you have established one brand, you can start other brands to diversify your sales. Each additional niche will provide an additional layer of stability to your business.

The wonderful thing about this business model is that it easily automated. There are a large number of tasks to bring a product to market but many of them can be done by a virtual assistant. As you grow and expand, hiring a virtual assistant from Upwork may make sense for you to rapidly grow the brand.

A million-dollar business
Let's say that each product averages a $10 profit margin.

Let's say that each product sells 20 units a day.

$1,000,000 profit per year / $10 average profit margin = 100,000 units per year

100,000 units per year / 12 months / 30 days = 277 units per day

277 units per day / 20 units per day for each product = about 14 different products

It may take 6 months to finally be able to roll out your second product, and another couple of months to roll out your third. But after that you should be able to add at least one product per month. If you keep moving this business forward, the sky's the limit! Within 2 years it is not unreasonable to have built your own

PRIVATE LABEL EMPIRE!

Appendix 1

90 Day Action Plan
Week 1
1.   Open an Amazon.com Seller account. I recommend opening a Merchant Fulfilled account to start (because there is no monthly cost) so that you can see how to make a listing, etc. After you are ready to order, switch it to a professional account ($40/month)

2.   Get the Jungle Scout Chrome extension

3.   Try to make a list of 20-30 product ideas.

Week 2
1.   Open an Alibaba account. Also Global Sources. Thomas Net, etc.

2.   Start adding products to your favorites, and make folders for each.

3.   Pick 10 to 20 potential suppliers.

4.   Send introduction email.

Week 3
1.   Order samples.

2.   Research the competitor's listings and reviews.

3.   Pick a Company Name

4.   Check the Domain is available

5.   Get a logo made on fiverr.

Week 4
1.   Review the samples.

2.   Request any modifications.

3.   Make a final decision as to the supplier you will choose.

4.   Create packaging with logo.

Week 5
1.   Order MOQ of products.

2.   Create listing.

3.   Use your sample product to get unverified reviews from a few friends.

Week 6 and 7
1.   Continue getting reviews while waiting for the shipment to reach FBA

2.   Set up your review system with feedbackgenius or salesbacker

Week 8
1.   After shipment has reached FBA, start launch process.

2.   Get 15 to 20 reviews from friends and family, tomoson, or reviewkick.

3.   Turn on PPC

4.   Do a promotional giveaway.

Weeks 9-12

1.   Continually keeping striving for more sales and reviews.

2.   Refine the listing once per week.

3.   Order more product

Appendix 2 Resources

Youtube videos

This is the introduction video for Oct 2014 ASM 4. It gives a great introduction to the business and discusses the Profit Spotlight 2.0 tool

https://www.youtube.com/watch?v=uuv6GT-fORo

This is a bonus video by Amazing Selling Machine when they launched ASM 4. In it they discuss how to pick products.

https://www.youtube.com/watch?v=u1OoOxy8v5w

In this video Ryan Moran, who is part of ASM, and leader of "the tribe" presents how to launch a product.

https://www.youtube.com/watch?v=JxXLQ5YzRec

This next video is the second time Ryan presents at the ASM conference, in which he expands on what they have learned in the tribe and how to grow an Amazon business from nothing to $1 million dollars in a year. It is a very informative and inspiring video.

https://www.youtube.com/watch?v=-Y35mxePPCc

These next 3 video are an interview of Matt Clark of Amazing Selling Machine by Stefan Pylarinos of Project Life Mastery (one of my favorite blogs). In this interview, Matt answers all the questions about the business.

https://www.youtube.com/watch?v=hGvlamkq2GY

https://www.youtube.com/watch?v=-BKaKhuKdsQ

https://www.youtube.com/watch?v=Yxve0ArR6z8

In addition to these that I have linked, I would also suggest following Ryan Moran's Tribe meetings on YouTube. Search "Ryan Moran Tribe" and you will find past episodes.

Podcasts
Freedom Fast Lane by Ryan Daniel Moran - Search episodes from Summer/Fall of 2014

Smart Passive Income – Pat Flynn –

The Amazing Seller – Scott Voelker – Dedicated just to Private Label FBA

The Private Labeler Show- Nick Landowski

Private Label Empire Builders – Kevin Rizer

AMPMpodcast – Manny Coats

Email Follow-up
www.salesbacker.com

www.feedbackgenius.com

Keyword and Product searches
www.merchantwords.com

www.keywordinspector.com

www.camelcamelcamel.com/

www.scientificseller.com

www.helium10.com

Launching a product
www.zonblast.com

www.viral-launch.com

www.tomoson.com

www.reviewkick.com

Community
Facebook - Amazon FBA Private Label Sellers

Facebook- The Amazing Seller

Facebook – FBA High Rollers

Reddit- http://www.reddit.com/r/FulfillmentByAmazon/

Website / Email

www.bluehost.com

www.mailchimp.com

www.aweber.com

Other

http://www.taxjar.com/

http://cheap-upc-barcode.com/

www.chinaimportal.com

Conclusion

I hope that you have found this guide useful.

This business is certainly not a get rich quick scheme. It will take time and dedication on your part to learn the ins and outs of the process. But with constant effort, you will be able to get over any hurdles that stand in your way, and build a successful business in a relatively short amount of time.

I spent hours researching all the information to learn this business. and I wanted to share what I have learned. With this book, it is my hope that the learning curve is quicker for you.

If you have enjoyed it and found it helpful, PLEASE LEAVE A POSITIVE REVIEW.

Reviews are HUGE on Amazon ;)

Thank you!

41566914R00050

Made in the USA
Middletown, DE
16 March 2017